I Like Science! Bilingual

En busca de **tormentas** con un **científico**

Searching for **STORMS** with a **Scientist**

Judith Williams

Enslow Elementary
an imprint of
Enslow Publishers, Inc.

40 Industrial Road
Box 398
Berkeley Heights, NJ 07922
USA
http://ww.enslow.com

Contents

Contenido

Words to Know/Palabras a conocer

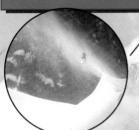

blizzard (BLIZ urd)—Cold weather with snow and strong winds. There is
blowing snow it is hard to se...
la ventisca—Clima frío con nieve y vientos fuertes. Hay tanta nieve en el v...
es difícil ver bien.

forecast (FOR cast)—A report that tells what the weather will be like.
el pronóstico—Un inter... el clima.

hail (HAYL)—Small pie...
el granizo—Pequeños ped...

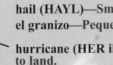

hurricane (HER ih cayn)—A lar... ... ...
to land.
el huracán—Una gran tormen... ... ...éano y puede...
tierra firme.

meteorologist (meet ee or AH toh jist)—A scientist who studies the weather.
el meteorólogo—Un científico que estudia el clima.

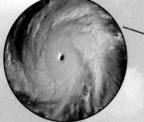

severe (sa VEER) weather—Bad and sometimes unsafe weather.
el clima severo—Mal clima que a veces es peligroso.

tornado (tor NAY doh)—A strong twisting wind below a thunderstorm that touches
the ground.
el tornado—Un viento fuerte en forma de torbellino que se presenta debajo de una
tormenta eléctrica y toca el suelo.

What is weather?

Weather is sunny days, rainy nights, windy mornings, and snowy afternoons.

Scientists learn about weather to keep us safe. What an important job!

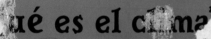

Los científicos estudian el clima para protegernos. ¡Es un trabajo muy importante!

3

Meet meteorologist Harold Brooks.

He is a weather scientist.

He learns about severe weather, like strong winds, hail, and thunderstorms.

Él es el meteorólogo Harold Brooks.

Es científico del clima.

Él estudia el clima severo, como los vientos fuertes, el granizo y las tormentas eléctricas.

4

Why does this weather sometimes start tornadoes? Where? When? These are questions he asks about storms.

¿Por qué este clima a veces inicia tornados? ¿Dónde? ¿Cuándo? Éstas son preguntas que él hace acerca de las tormentas.

What is a weather forecast?

Meteorologists watch weather maps on computers. The maps show the changing weather. Is it wet? Is it windy or hot?

¿Qué es el pronóstico del clima?

Los meteorólogos observan mapas del clima en computadoras. Los mapas muestran los cambios en el clima. ¿Hay humedad? ¿Hay viento o calor?

6

These answers help meteorologists make a forecast. The forecast tells us what the weather will be.

Estas respuestas ayudan a los meteorólogos a hacer un pronóstico. El pronóstico nos dice cómo estará el clima.

What is a weather watch?

Meteorologists see that severe weather, like hail, might happen where you live. Watch the sky! Is it getting dark?

It might be time for a weather warning.

¿Qué es una vigilancia climatológica?

Los meteorólogos ven si el clima severo, como el granizo, puede presentarse en el lugar donde tú vives. ¡Observa el cielo! ¿Se está poniendo oscuro?

Pudiera ser hora de una advertencia climatológica.

What is a weather warning?

A weather warning tells us that severe weather has started. Be sure to go to a safe place.

hail on the ground/ granizo en el suelo

¿Qué es una advertencia climatológica?

hail/granizo

Una advertencia climatológica nos dice que el clima severo ha iniciado. Ve a un lugar seguro.

Is there ever a snow watch or warning?

Yes. People need to be ready for lots of snow.

¿Existe una vigilancia o advertencia de nevadas?

Sí. Las personas necesitan prepararse cuando va a nevar mucho.

Sometimes the weather gets really cold and there are high winds and snow. This is called a blizzard.

A veces el clima se pone muy frío y hay vientos fuertes y nieve. A eso se le llama ventisca.

Is there severe weather on the ocean?

Yes. Huge ocean storms in North America are called **hurricanes**.

¿Existe clima severo en el océano?

Sí. Las enormes tormentas oceánicas en Norteamérica se llaman **huracanes**.

If a hurricane moves onto land,
the wind can blow down
buildings. Heavy rain and big
waves can start floods.

Si un huracán avanza hasta tierra firme,
el viento puede derribar edificios. La
lluvia fuerte y las grandes olas pueden
causar inundaciones.

What severe weather happens the most?

Thunderstorms! They have rain, wind, thunder, and lightning. Sometimes hail falls with the rain.

¿Qué clima severo se presenta con más frecuencia?

¡Las tormentas eléctricas! Tienen lluvia, viento, truenos y relámpagos. En ocasiones junto con la lluvia cae granizo.

14

Meteorologists watch carefully.
They look for clues that a tornado
could start.

Los meteorólogos observan
cuidadosamente. Buscan pistas de qué
podría iniciar un tornado.

1.

cool air/aire frío

warm air/aire caliente

rain/lluvia

How do thunderstorms start tornadoes?

1. Thunderstorms start when warm, wet air rises high into the sky. This makes clouds.

2. The wind under a storm cloud blows hard. The air on the ground moves slower. This makes the wind in between roll like a long tube.

3. Sometimes the warm air lifts one end of the spinning tube up into the cloud.

4. As the wind, rain, and air around the tube touch the ground, a tornado can be formed.

2.

fast wind/
viento rápido

3.

4.

slow wind/viento lento

¿Cómo se inician los tornados debido a tormentas eléctricas?

1. Las tormentas eléctricas empiezan cuando el aire caliente y húmedo sube al cielo. Con eso se forman nubes.

2. El viento debajo de una nube de tormenta sopla fuerte. El aire del suelo se mueve más lentamente. Eso hace que el viento intermedio ruede como un tubo largo.

3. A veces el aire caliente levanta hacia la nube un extremo del tubo que va rodando.

4. Cuando el viento, la lluvia y el aire alrededor del tubo tocan la tierra, puede formarse un tornado.

How does meteorologist Harold learn about tornadoes?

He studies past storms. He puts these facts into a computer. The facts make a model.

The colors help show where storms might start. This computer model helps Harold see how storms are going to move.

Los colores ayudan a mostrar donde pueden iniciar las tormentas. Este modelo de computadora ayuda a Harold a ver cómo se mueven n las tormentas.

¿Cómo se entera el meteorólogo Harold de los tornados?

Estudia las tormentas pasadas. Pone estos datos en una computadora. Los datos hacen un modelo.

Models run like a computer
game. They show why some
storms start tornadoes. These
facts help forecast new
tornadoes around the world.

Los modelos funcionan como un juego
de computadora. Muestran por qué
algunas tormentas inician tornados.
Estos datos ayudan a pronosticar
nuevos tornados en todo el mundo.

Early storm warnings are important.
By learning about severe weather,
scientists help save lives. Thank you,
meteorologist Harold, for watching
the weather for us.

Las advertencias al inicio de una tormenta
son importantes. Estudiando el clima severo,
los científicos ayudan a salvar vidas. Gracias,
meteorólogo Harold, por observar el clima
por nosotros.

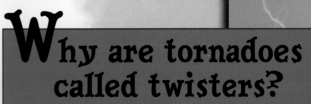

You will need:

✔ empty plastic soda bottle
   with a lid
✔ warm water
✔ dishwashing soap
✔ glitter

1. Fill a soda bottle halfway
   with warm water. Add a
   drop of dishwashing soap
   and a bit of glitter.

2. Put the top on tightly. Face a sunny
   window. Shake the bottle in circles
   many times.

3. Hold the bottle up toward the sunny
   window. Do you see the twister? The wind
   of a tornado spins almost the same way.

¿Por qué a los tornados se les llama torbellinos?

Necesitarás:

- ✔ botella de plástico de refresco vacía con tapa
- ✔ agua tibia
- ✔ jabón para lavar platos
- ✔ brillantina

1. Llena una botella de refresco hasta la mitad con agua tibia. Añade una gota de jabón para lavar platos y un poco de brillantina.

2 Cierra muy bien la botella. Colócate frente a una ventana por donde entre el sol. Agita la botella en círculos muchas veces.

3. Sostén la botella hacia la ventana. ¿Ves el torbellino? El viento de un tornado gira casi de la misma manera.

Learn More/ Más para aprender

Books / Libros

In English / En inglés

Berger, Melvin and Gilda. *Do Tornadoes Really Twist?*
New York: Scholastic Inc., 2000.

Knapp, Brian. *Weather Watch*. Danbury, Conn.: Grolier
Educational, 2000.

Michaels, Pat. *W is for Wind: A Weather Alphabet.*
Chelsea, MI: Sleeping Bear Press, 2005.

In Spanish / En inglés y español

Saunders-Smith, Gail. *Los relámpagos*. Mankato, Minn.:
Capstone Press, 2004.

Saunders-Smith, Gail. *Las nubes*. Mankato, Minn.:
Capstone Press, 2004.

Internet Addresses / Direcciones de Internet

In English / En inglés
National Weather Service: Storm Prediction Center
<http://www.spc.noaa.gov>

In English and Spanish / En inglés y español
Web Weather for Kids
<http://www.ucar.edu/educ_outreach/webweather/index.html>

Index

Índice

Series Literacy Consultant:
Allan A. De Fina, Ph.D.
Past President of the New Jersey Reading Association
Professor, Department of Literacy Education
New Jersey City University

Science Consultant:
Philip J. Currie, Ph.D., Curator of Dinosaur Research
Royal Tyrrell Museum, Alberta, Canada
Dr. Currie says, "I wish there had been a book like this when I was young!"

Note to Teachers and Parents: The *I Like Science!* series supports the National Science Education Standards for K- science, including content standards "Science as a human endeavor" and "Science as inquiry." The Words to Know section introduces subject-specific vocabulary, including pronunciation and definitions. Early readers may require hel with these new words.

Enslow Elementary, an imprint of Enslow Publishers, Inc.
Enslow Elementary® is a registered trademark of Enslow Publishers, Inc.

Bilingual edition copyright 2009 by Enslow Publishers, Inc. Originally published in English under the title *Searching for Storm Weather with a Scientist* © 2004 by Enslow Publishers, Inc. Bilingual edition translated by Nora Díaz of Strictly Spanish, LLC., edite by Strictly Spanish, LLC.

Library of Congress Cataloging-in-Publication Data

Williams, Judith (Judith A.)
  [Searching for storms with a scientist. Spanish & English]
  En busca de tormentas con un científico = Searching for storms with a scientist / Judith Williams.—Bilingual ed.
    p. cm.—(I like science! Bilingual)
    Summary: "Discusses severe weather"—Provided by publisher.
    Includes bibliographical references and index.
    ISBN-13: 978-0-7660-2980-4
    ISBN-10: 0-7660-2980-8
    1. Meteorology—Juvenile literature. I. Title.
QC863.5.W5518 2008
551.55vdc22   2007011592

Printed in the United States of America

10 9 8 7 6 5 4 3 2 1

Enslow Publishers, Inc., is committed to printing our books or recycled paper. The paper in every book contains 10% to 30% post-consumer waste (PCW). The cover board on the outside of each book contains 100% PCW. Our goal is to do our part to help young people and the environment too!

To Our Readers: We have done our best to make sure all Interne Addresses in this book were active and appropriate when we went to press. However, the author and the publisher have no control over and assume no liability for the material available on those Internet sites or on other Web sites they may link to. Any comments or suggestions can be sent by e-mail to comments@ enslow.com or to the address on the back cover.

Photo Credits: © David Cavagnaro/Visuals Unlimited, p. 7; © Jeff J. Daly/Visuals Unlimited, p. 9 (inset); © Charles A. Doswell III/Visuals Unlimited, pp. 14, 19;

Enslow Publishers, Inc., pp. 21, 22; © Marc Epstein/Visuals Unlimited, p. 13; © Joseph L. Fontenot/Visuals Unlimited, p. 3 (top); © Carlyn Galati/Visuals Unlimited, p. 9; © Joe McDonald/Visuals Unlimited, pp. 10-11; NASA, p. 2 (center); NOAA, p. 12; NOAA Photo Library, NOAA Central Library; OAR/National Severe Storms Lab, p. 15; NSSL, pp. 4, 20; NOAA/Storm Prediction Center, p. 18; © Gene Rhoden/Visuals Unlimited, p. 5; © Mark A. Schneider/Visuals Unlimited, p. 8; © Michael W. Skrepnick, pp. 16, 17; © Tom Uhlman/Visuals Unlimited, p. 6; © Visuals Unlimited, p. 3 (bottom).

Cover Photo: © A & J Verkaik/CORBIS